ROMAN DURHAM

by

FRANK GRAHAM

© 1979

I.S.B.N. 0 85983 155 8

Northern History Booklet No. 85

Published by Frank Graham
6 Queen's Terrace, Newcastle upon Tyne NE2 2PL

Printed by R. Ward & Sons Ltd.
Dunston, Gateshead, Tyne & Wear

CONTENTS

	page
The Roads	3
Miscellaneous Finds	5
Old Durham Bathhouse	6
Piercebridge	7
Binchester	10
Lanchester	17
Ebchester	22
Chester-le-Street	27
South Shields	29

The old maps used in this book are by
Henry Maclauchan — 1852

The illustrations on pages 32 and 35 are by kind
permission of Tyne and Wear Museum Service.

Several of the maps and drawings are by
E. Dale and D. S. Thompson.

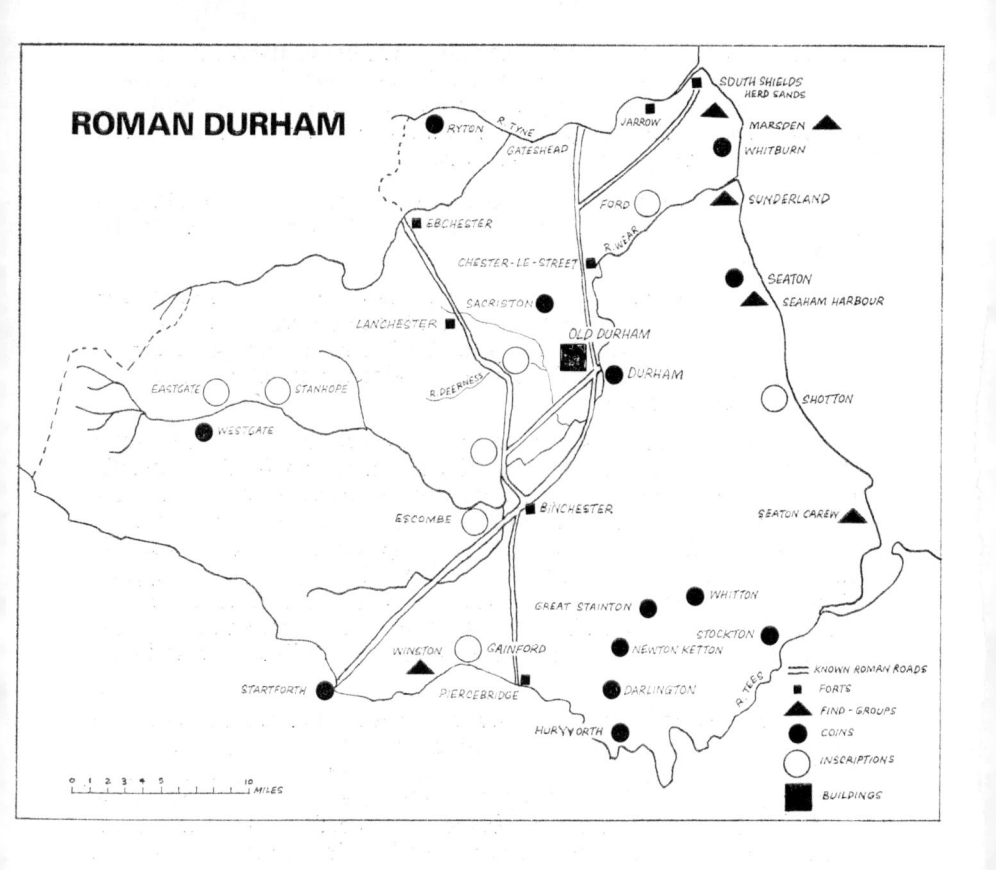

ROMAN DURHAM

There was a great difference between North and South Britain in Roman times. The south was purely civilian whereas the north was a military zone. However even on the Roman Wall there were civilian settlements and in Durham we can assume there were many people engaged in agriculture and trade. However, due to the small amount of excavation that has taken place we have only a limited knowledge of the position in Durham during Roman times. Of the six Roman forts in the county only South Shields has been extensively excavated. Even the Roman roads are obscure.

The Roads

There was one certain road through the county running from Piercebridge through Binchester, Lanchester, and Ebchester to the Roman town of Corbridge. It was called *Deor* Street by Symeon of Durham. Today the name Dere Street and Watling Street are both in use. This road has been uncovered at various points along its route. Hutchinson in the late 18th century describes a stretch he saw south of Ebchester:

We paid great attention to the great Roman road which leads to this place from the southward and found it remarkably perfect where the

3

new inclosures of common lands had not taken place. We traced it for a considerable distance, so as to ascertain the dimensions. It is formed in three distinct parts, with four ditches: a centre road probably for carriages and cavalry, forty-two feet wide with a narrow road on each side for foot passengers, twelve feet wide.

(For a full description of this road in Northumberland and Durham see *Dere Street. Roman Road North. From York to Scotland.* T. H. Rowland. 1974).

Many other Roman roads in Durham have been suggested at one time and another but only now is concrete evidence becoming available. A road parallel to Dere Street from York passing through Durham City and reaching Newcastle has been claimed but not a single yard of it has been uncovered.

The *Bowes-Bishop Auckland* road has now been shown to exist. John Warburton, Horsley, Hutchinson, MacLaughlan and W. D. Longstaffe had all written about it giving details of sections they knew but until field research was carried out in 1936 (see A.A. 1937. R. P. Wright) their statements could only be considered conjectural. The road was excavated at three different sites in Durham showing it to be a typical Roman feat of engineering, its width varying from 22 to 24 feet. It crossed the Tees at Startforth and followed an almost straight course for Dere Street which it joined three miles south of Binchester at Burns House.

Binchester seems to have been a road junction. Besides the road from Bowes (*Lavatrae*) another branch road led to the north-east, possibly as far as Chester-le-Street. This road was uncovered at various spots in 1937 (A.A. 1938. R. P. Wright). It left Dere Street just west of the colliery village of Willington, passed Brancepeth Colliery and Park House making for Stone Bridge near Neville's Cross. Beyond this point the road has not been traced but it seems a reasonable conjecture that after crossing the Deerness and Browney valleys the road would head north for Chester-le-Street.

A Roman road ran from *Durham to Newcastle*. This road almost followed the line of the main A1 road to Newcastle. Only where it left the latter road could it be traced. This happens north of Birtley where the Roman road runs on the east side of the A1 near the Coach and Horses Inn and then on the west side near High Eighton. Here it was found to be 17½ feet wide with kerbs. At Wrekenton a branch led off to South Shields. The Durham-Newcastle road took the highest ground near Beacon Lough then turned west off north. It followed the line of Gateshead High Street to the Roman bridge of Pons Aelius (Newcastle). It did not continue north of the Wall.

South Shields was an important supply base and it was joined to the Roman road network by the *Wrekendyke*. This was a special branch road which left the Durham-Newcastle road at Wrekenton. It ran north east to keep to the higher ground but when close to the fort on the Lawe turned more to the north. Near Wrekenton it has been examined and was found to be 19 feet wide with a four inch layer of large stones as a foundation covered by a layer of small sandstones with a kerb formed from 12 inch sandstone blocks. Where it is crossed by the main

Newcastle-Sunderland road it can still be seen well raised and overgrown with bushes. It passes through Monkton and Primrose.

Miscellaneous Finds.

Roman objects have been found in various parts of Durham. They prove the existence of a Romanized civilian population but an individual find does not prove the existence of a Roman building in the vicinity. Near Stanhope in Weardale was found an altar to *Silvanus* erected by Caius Tetius Veturius Micianus, a cavalry commander in the Roman army. He set it up gladly "for taking a wild boar of remarkable fineness

SILVANO INVICTO SAC[RVM]
C[AIVS] TETIVS VETVRIVS MICIA-
NVS PRAEF[ECTVS] ALAE SEBOSIA-
NAE OB APRVM EXIMIAE
FORMAE CAPTVM QVEM
MVLTI ANTECESSO-
RES EIVS PRAEDARI
NON POTVERVNT V. S. L. M.

To Silvanus the invincible sacred Caius Tetius Veturius Micianus prefect of the Sebosian cavalry on account of a boar of enormous size taken which many of his predecessors were not able to destroy [erected this] in discharge of a vow.

Size, 3 feet by 1 foot 3 inches.

which many of his predecessors had been unable to bag". From Eastgate, higher up the dale, another altar to the same deity was erected by one Aurelius Quirinus. Other Roman objects—an amphora, two skillets and coins have been found in the area but they do not prove the Romans had permanent settlements here and nothing has been found to show they worked the lead mines of Weardale.

5

When the danger of raiders from across the North Sea threatened the coast the Romans built fortified signal stations. There were several in Yorkshire, the most northerly being at Huntcliff near Saltburn. None have been traced in Durham. Around Sunderland discoveries of Roman objects have been made but nothing of importance.

In 1940 an accidental discovery at Old Durham provided new evidence about Roman civilisation in the county.

Old Durham Bathhouse

The farmhouse at Old Durham lies less than one mile east of Durham. The site has attracted antiquaries for a long time chiefly because of the fine prehistoric promontory fort, called Maiden Castle, on the opposite bank of the Wear. However a Roman fort had been suggested for the site early in the 19th century. In 1940 a building was found a quarter of a mile south of the old farmhouse. Excavations revealed a fine domestic bath-house but the villa to which it belonged could not be traced although trial trenches were dug. That it was a Romanized farmstead is beyond doubt. It must have been large and important to have the amenity of a bath-house. It is the most northerly Roman farmstead in the Roman Empire. The nearest known Roman domestic building is in Yorkshire at Middleham in Wensleydale. The discovery at Old Durham suggests the possibility of further discoveries elsewhere in Durham. (For detailed report see A.A. 1944).

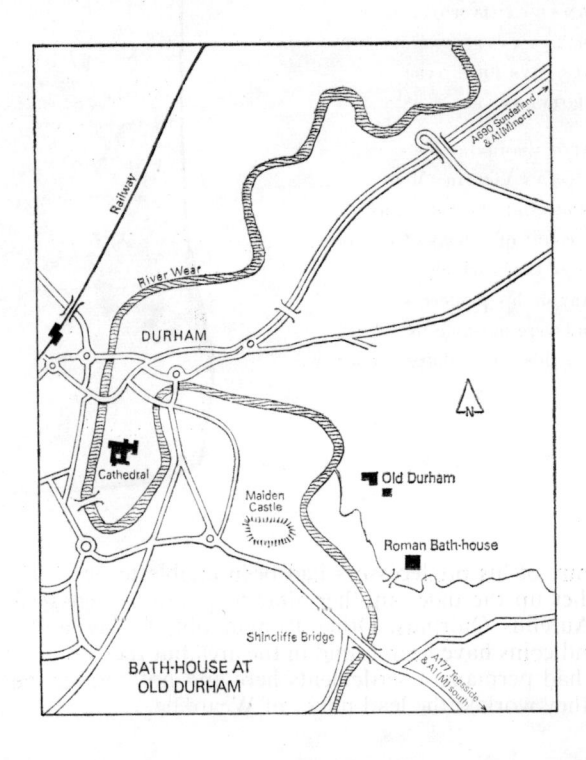

BATH-HOUSE AT OLD DURHAM

PIERCEBRIDGE

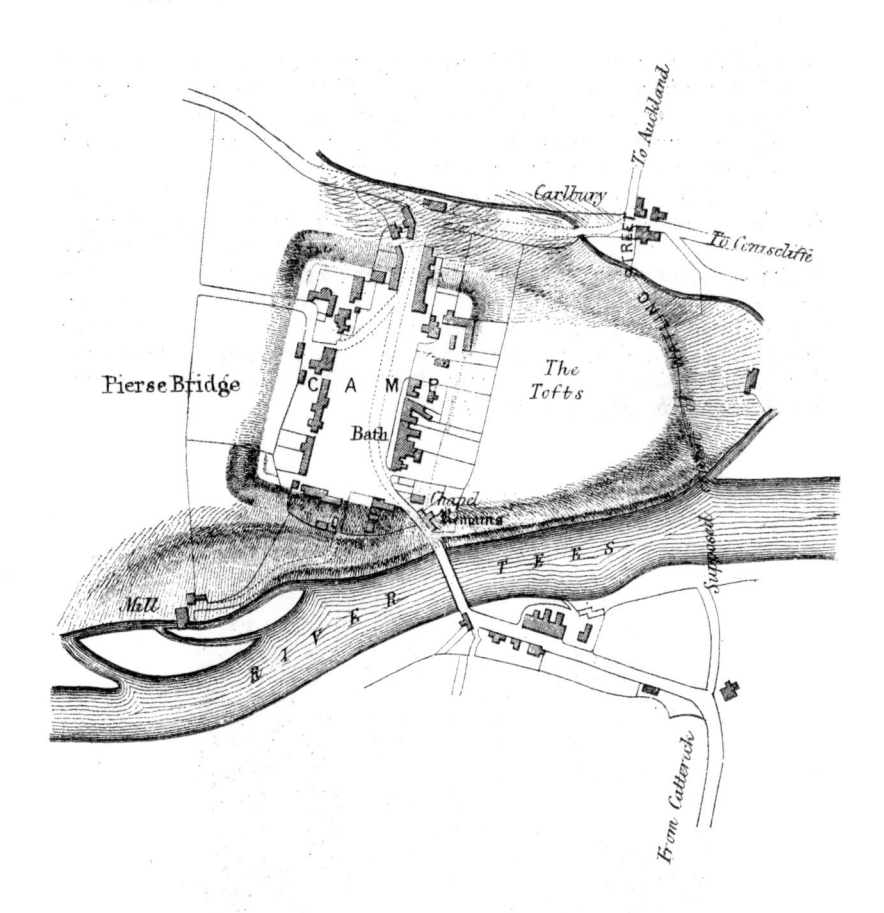

Piercebridge is a small village grouped around the village green. Most parts of the village lies within the ramparts of the Roman fort. It lies on the Roman road of Dere Street which crossed the river Tees 260 yards downstream from the present bridge. Recent gravel workings have exposed the stonework. Some years ago oak piles, probably from the original bridge, were found here. Horsley was the first to describe the site in detail.

> This place has been a considerable Roman station. A larger number of coins have been found here. An aqueduct, if I am not mistaken, has gone just through the present town, and the foundations of houses every where appear, especially when the earth is any way opened, or even well watered with rain, and after a shower the coins are also discovered and gathered up in abundance. A large stone coffin was also found here, and other antiquities. The last time I viewed the place, I was inclined to think that a sort of garden, with some trees in it, which I once imagined might be inclosed in part with some of the ramparts of the station, has rather been the praetorium only. This station and town are on the north side of the Tees; but there is a rivulet on the north side of the station; so that it had

7

the usual situation on a lingula between a greater and a smaller river, and near their confluence; yet there is high ground both to the north and south of the station. As I went from Durham to Piersbridge I saw two seeming tumuli, one a mile from the town on the left, the other near the entrance to the town on the right. The military way from Binchester to this place is very visible, especially near Piersbridge; my landlord called it the Broadway. He also told me of a bridge, some of the wood of which was yet remaining: there was an elevation very visible beyond this bridge (which was over the rivulet); but I took this place to be rather the continuance of the military way than any part of the ramparts of the station. The way points directly to the Tofts, the field in which the station has probably been, and from which the coins have the name of toft-pieces. The houses which stand here are called the Bury, or Carlbury. I take Piersbridge to be Magae in the Notitia.

[*I(ovi)*] *o(ptimo) m(aximo) Dolycheno* [*I*]*ul(ius) Valentin*[*us*], *ord(inatus) Ger(mania) su*[*p(eriori)*], *ex iussu ipsiu*[*s*] *posuit pro se* [*et*] *suis* . . .

"Julius Valentinus, centurion, from Upper [Southern] Germany, erected this altar to Juppiter Dolychenus at his own command."

Hutchinson says the "Roman road passed a few paces east of the station . . . . an ancient bridge over the river lay in this direction; the timbers, piles or framings of the foundation were visible till the great flood in November, 1771, when they were torn up and washed away".

The civilian settlement was in the area of the Tofts and chance finds show it dates back to Hadrian's time. It has been suggested this is a unique case in the north of a large civilian settlement establishing itself on a busy Roman road before a fort was built. However as yet we have not uncovered the full history of the fort here. The present fort of about 300 A.D. was probably moved from an earlier site. It is very large covering over ten acres and was probably built or rebuilt by the 6th Legion as a fragment of a stone dedication testifies. In 1939 Dere Street was excavated here. Originally it seems to have been Agricolan and was twice rebuilt. Its width was 27 feet.

The road through the village today is roughly on the line of the fort's *via principalis*. The ramparts are visible on all sides with a ditch probably on the west. Sites for a bath and aqueduct have been found but are no longer visible. The only exposed parts of the fort are in the northeast corner. They show bits of the wall, barracks and a sewer. The cemetery seems to have been north of the fort where burials have been found. In the same area evidence of Roman industrial activity, including a lime kiln, was revealed. The church at Gainford two miles away is built of Roman stones. The dedication on previous page was found at Piercebridge.

But the finest object found at Piercebridge is illustrated here. It is now in the British Museum and is a small bronze statuette showing a ploughman with a light wheelless plough called the *aratrum*, a type used all over the Roman Empire.

A bronze statuette from Piercebridge

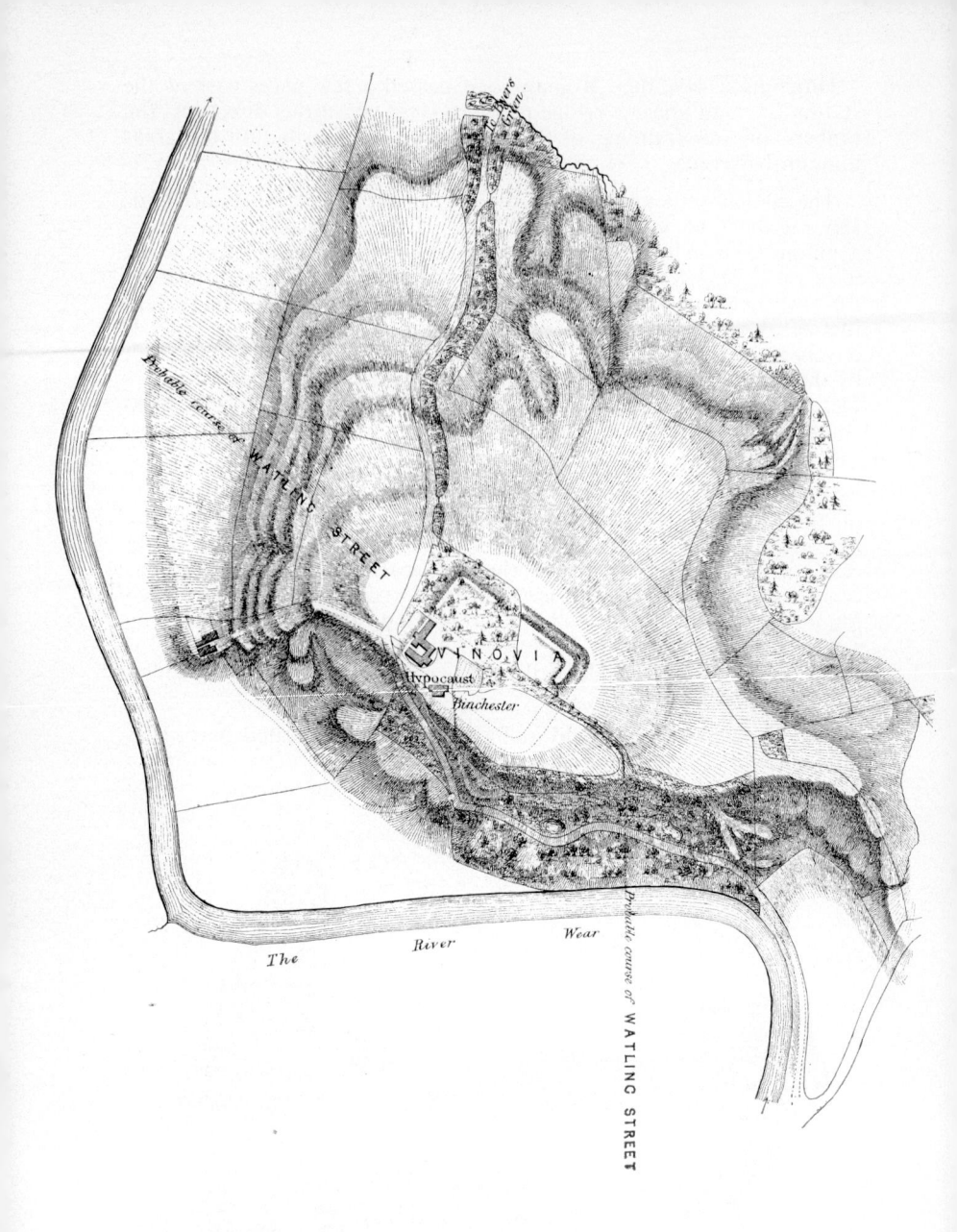

BINCHESTER (Vinovia)

Binchester is the next station on Dere Street north of Piersbridge from which it is distant about ten miles. The camp is on a hill top, almost encircled by the river Wear north of Bishop Auckland. The Roman name was Vinovia and the garrison, although often changed, appears to have been usually cavalry. Many inscriptions and monuments have been found here at various times but few have survived.

There was a fine Elizabethan Hall on the site of the fort. But when the estate passed into the hands of Van Mildert, the Bishop of Durham the mansion was demolished and all the altars and monuments which had been collected and preserved with care in the courtyard "were used in forming the 'stoppings' of a neighbouring coal pit". The following altar was rescued at the pit's mouth.

Fortunae sanctae M. Val(erius) Fulvianu[s] praef(ectus) eq(uitum) v(otum) s(olvit) l(ibens) l(aetus) m(erito).

"M. Valerius Fulvianus, commander of cavalry [*i.e.,* of the cavalry in garrison at Binchester], pays his vow to Fortune."

MacLaughlan was able to trace the north and east ramparts and estimated the size as 214 yards by 160 yards making about seven acres.

A perfect altar was found in a field south of the fort. The reading is:—

I(OVI) O(PTIMO) M(AXIMO) | ET MATRIB | VS OLLOTO | TIS SIVE TRA | NSMARINIS | POMPONIVS DONATVS | B(ENE)F(ICIARIVS) CO(N)S(VLARIS) PRO | SALVTE SVA | ET SVORVM | V(OTVM) S(OLVIT) L(IBENTE) A(NIMO).

This means the altar was dedicated by Pomponius Donatus to Jupiter and the Overseas Mothers. The stone describes him as a *beneficiarius*, who was a military official employed on special services. He was probably the fort commander.

Binchester was built in the later part of the first century A.D. and was still occupied in the fourth century but much excavation will be necessary before its full history can be revealed.

The show piece is the baths of the Commandant's house, accidently discovered in 1815 and now fully excavated and consolidated for the Department of the Environment. It is the most perfect hypocaust in the north of England. When first found there were 88 pillars (11 rows with 8 in each row). Each pillar consisted of some 16 tiles. One pillar was removed by a vandal but 87 still stand (although some are restored). The furnace flues can be seen.

An interesting votive tablet found at Binchester and now in the Cathedral Library at Durham, is illustrated below.

[AES]CVLAPIO
[ET]SALVTI
[PRO SALV]TE ALAE VET
[TONVM·] C·R·M· AVRE
[L·GLOSS]OCOMAS·ME
[V·S·] L·M·

Expanded:—

AESCULAPIO ET SALUTI,
PRO SALUTE ALAE VETTONUM,
CIVIUM ROMANORUM,
MARCUS AURELIUS GLOSSOCOMAS,
MEDICUS,
VOTUM SOLVIT LIBENS MERITO
(or? MERITIS).

The god Aesculapius holds his daughter by his right hand, while in his left he carries a stout staff round which is twined a serpent. The inscription translated reads: *To Aesculapius and Salus, for the health of all of the Vettonians, Roman citizens, Mareus Aurelius . . . . ocomas, physician, willingly discharges a vow.* Another altar carries a dedication: *To the transmarine mothers, the cavalry of the Ala of the Vettonians, Roman citizens, willingly have discharged a vow.*

These two altars show that the cavalry of the Ala of Vettonians were stationed here.

Dere Street probably crossed the Wear to the west of the fort. Leland mentions an "exceeding fair bridge of one arch upon the Were". MacLaughlan's plan shows Dere Street crossing the river twice. This is very unlikely. To avoid building two bridges the Romans would undoubtedly have diverted the road or perhaps the river has changed its course since the time of the Romans. There was a civilian settlement to the south of the fort. Houses were found on both sides of Dere Street as well as a bath house. The famous Saxon church of Escomb, a short distance away across the river was built almost entirely of Roman stones, the chancel arch having come direct from some Roman building.

·ESCOMB, S.E. VIEW.

Describing Escomb Church Charles Hodges mentions that "many of the ashlars are of very large size, and numerous indications of their former use are visible, such as cramp and lewis holes, broached tooling, fragments of inscriptions etc. It is mainly owing to this sound material, and especially to the huge blocks which form the quoins at the angles, that these high and thin walls have stood firm for ten centuries or more".

13

THE ROMAN HYPOCAUST AT BINCHESTER.

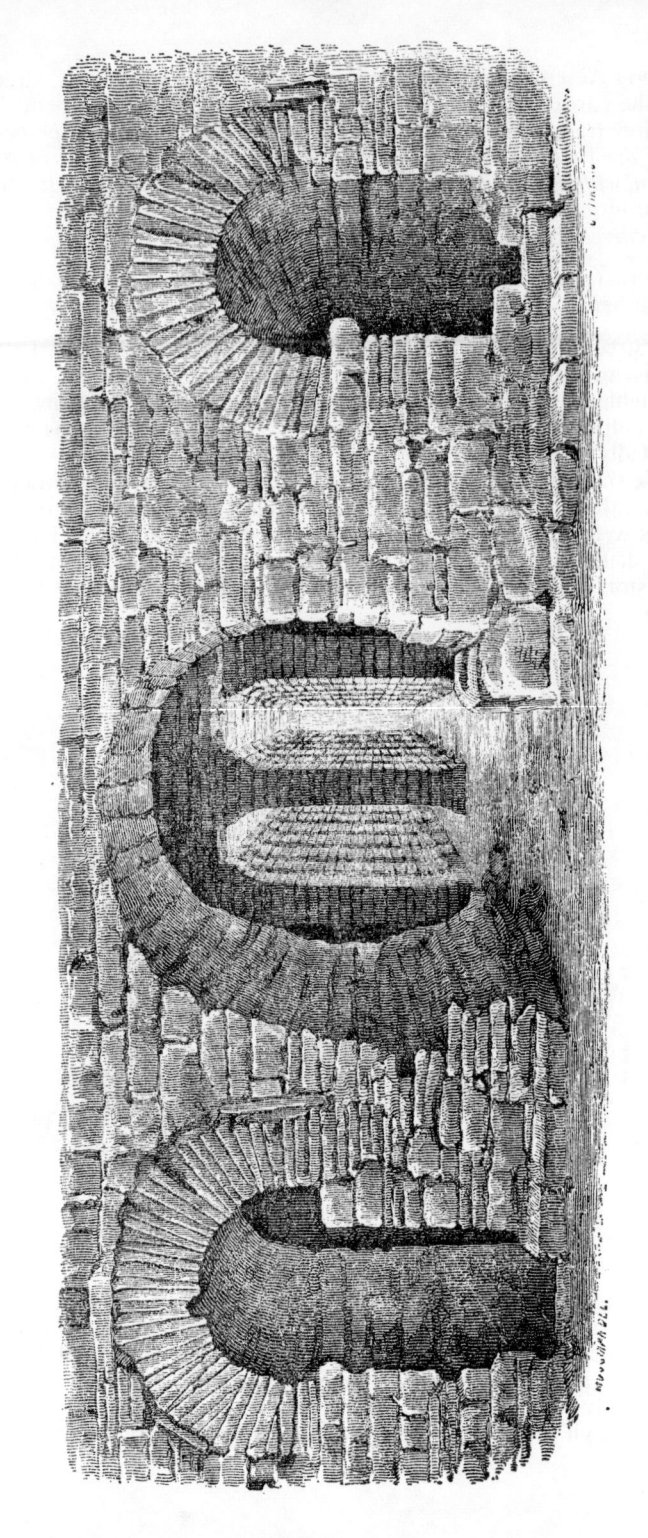

Height of the pillars, three feet five inches. Size of the tiles forming the shaft of the pillars, eight inches square by about two inches thick. Size of the tiles forming the base and the capital of the pillars, twelve inches square by about two inches and three-quarters thick. Size of the tiles forming the floor which rests upon the pillars, seventeen inches square by about three inches thick.

14

Corner of east rampart of Binchester. Excavated 1878.

Room above the hypocaust at Binchester.

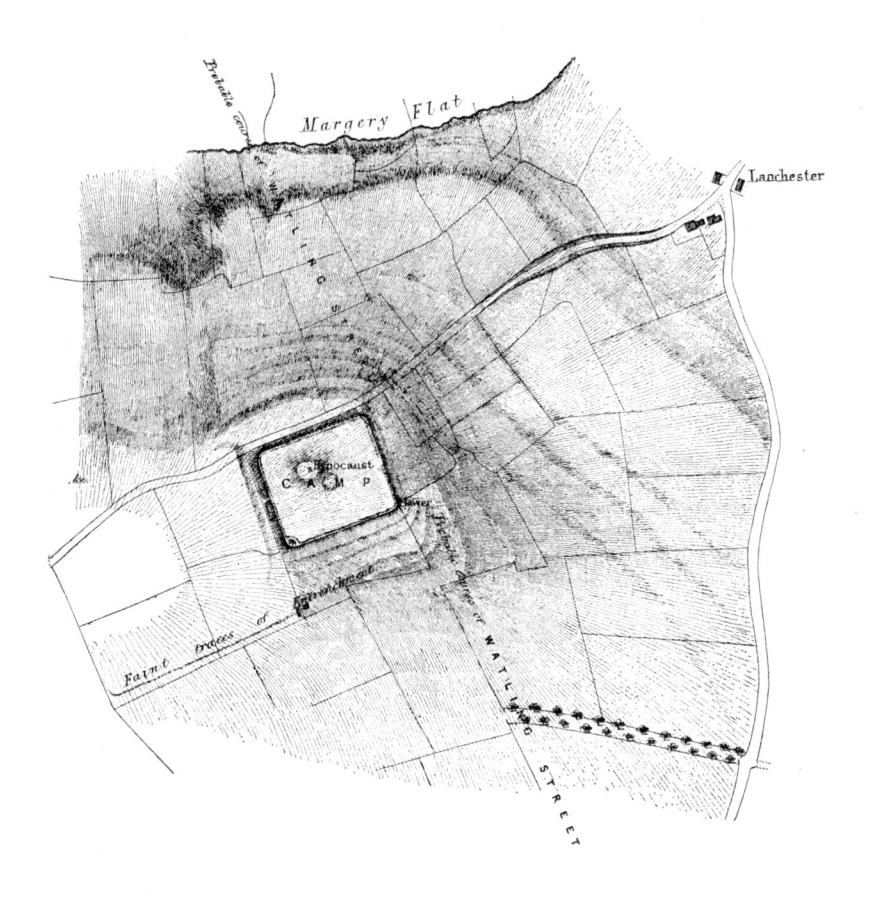

LANCHESTER (Longovicium)

The Roman camp here has never been properly excavated. At MacLaughlan remarked more than a century ago, "the interior is in pasture, and no doubt covers a rich mine of antiquities". It is a large fort and covers almost six acres measuring 188 yards north to south and 156 yards to east and west. It guards Dere Street which passed the fort on its east side. The Roman name was Longovicium. It was constructed about 140 A.D. and replaced Binchester and Ebchester in order to save manpower. The fort went out of use during the first half of the third century but was then restored and in the fourth century much rebuilding was carried out. During limited excavation in 1937 the walls were found to be nine feet thick at the base. Each side had double portals with guard towers. There were also corner and interval towers. The following stone probably stood above one of these gates. It shows two Victories supporting a wreath within which is an inscription telling us it was built by the Twentieth Legion, the Valerean and Victorious.

Size, 4 feet 6 inches by 2 feet.

Imp(erator) Caesar M. Antonius Gordianus p(ius) f(elix) Augustus principia et armamentaria conlapsa restituit per Maecilium Fuscum leg(atum) Aug(usti) pr(o) pr(aetore), curante M. Aur(elio) Quirino pr(aefecto) coh(ortis) i L(ingonum) Gor(dianae).

"The Emperor Gordianus restored the headquarters and armouries [of the fort] by the agency of Maecilius Fuscus, governor of the province; the work was supervised by M. Aurelius Quirinus, commander of the First cohort of Lingones."

18

Two fine inscriptions record the rebuilding of the baths, the headquarters and the armouries, about A.D. 238-244.

Imp(erator) Caes(ar) M. Ant(onius) Gordianus p(ius) f(elix) Aug(ustus) balneum cum basilica a [so]lo instruxit per Egn(atium) Lucilianum leg(atum) Aug(usti) pr(o)pr(aetore) curante M. Aur(elio) Quirino pr(a)ef(ecto) coh(ortis) i L(ingonum) G(ordianae).

"The Emperor Gordianus [the third of the name] erected a bath with a basilica by the agency of Egnatius Lucilianus, governor of the province; the work was supervised by M. Aurelius Quirinus, commander of the First cohort of Lingones, called Gordian, [then in garrison at Lanchester]."

An unusual and rare bi-lingual altar in Greek and Latin was found here. The garrison commander, the tribune T. Flavius Titianus erected it to the Greek god of healing Aesculapius.

[Aescula]pio T. Fl(avius) Titianus trib(unus) v(otum) s(olvit) l(ibens) l(aetus) m(erito).

['Ασκλη]πίῳ [Τίτος] Φλαύ[ι]ος Τιτιανο[ς] χ[ι]λίαρ[χ]ος.

The following two stones were probably parts of one monument.

GENIO PRAETORI[I]
CL. EPAPHRODITVS
CLAVDIANVS
TRIBVNVS C[O]HO[RTIS]
I. LING[ONVM] V.L.P.M.

To the genius of the prætorium
Claudius Epaphroditus
Claudianus
tribune of cohort the first
of the Lingones erected this willingly in discharge of a vow.

In a field next to the south west corner of the camp is a wet hollow which was once the reservoir providing a regular supply of water. Two aqueducts brought the water from four miles away, the two joining together half a mile from the reservoir. Near Hollinside Hall a narrow bank along the south side of the Wolsingham road shows the line of the south aqueduct. On the north aqueduct two streams were dammed to maintain the flow.

Along Dere Street to the north were the cemetery and signs of the civilian settlement. Of the internal buildings only the hypocaust of the Praetorium can be seen. On the north and east sides of the fort traces of extensive mounds and ditches are faintly visible.

Lanchester Church has many Roman stones in its fabric, especially the columns of the north arcade. In the south porch is a fine large Roman altar, over five feet high and weighing about three-quarters of a ton, dedicated to the British goddess Garmangabis. Possibly a temple to her stood in the vicinity where the altar was found, midway between the fort and the village of Lanchester. It is dated about 244. (A.A. 2.16). It is shown on the next page.

D MARTI
AVG
AVFFIDI D
VS AVFI
DIANVS

Marti
Augusto
Auffidi-
us Aufi-
dianus donum dat.

Actual Size.

This gold plate was found at Lanchester. Translated it reads: *Aufidius Aufidianus dedicates this to Mars*. It is of the same weight as two guineas. It was probably attached to an altar or an image of the god. The letters have been punched up from the under side; in one or two places the tool has gone through the metal. It is now in the Library of the Dean and Chapter, Durham.

21

EBCHESTER (Vindomora)

The first station south of the Tyne upon the line of Dere Street is Ebchester which is ten miles from Corbridge and seven miles from Lanchester. It is situated on a terrace above the river Derwent with a bold escarpment. On its western side the Ebchester burn forms a deep valley. The fort occupies a strong strategic site guarding the river crossing. It covers an area of four acres with the parish church and churchyard occupying the south-west angle. Its Roman name was Vindomora.

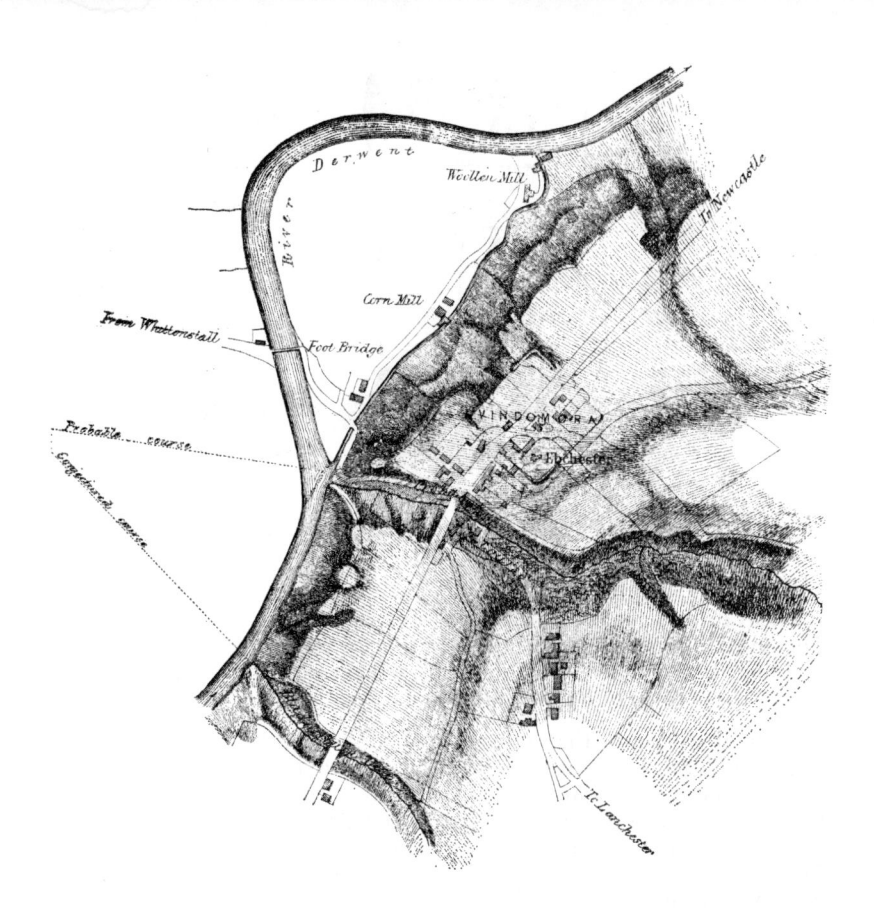

Bruce (1867) writes:

The walls of the station are taken down, but their foundations may be traced. The parish church, built of Roman stones, stands within it, near its south-west corner . . . . The modern turnpike road, between Newcastle and Shotley Bridge crosses the station from east to west, probably on the very line of its Via Principalis.

Surtees (1820) tells us:

The vallum and agger are most perfect on the north where they stretch along the very edge of the hill towards the river for a hundred and sixty paces. The north-west angle is perfect, and part of the western agger, though cut through by roads and foot-paths. On the south, also, the vallum is extremely distinguishable just within the southern wall of the church-yard.

DEO
VITIRI
MAXIMV
S V S

Deo
Vitiri
Maximu-
s votum solvit.

Size, 1 foot 4 inches by 8 inches.

An altar dedicated either to a local god Vitiris, or to "the ancient god".

Excavations have been piece-meal because the site site was built over. The most important were in 1972-3. They revealed four periods of building with wooden structures, all of them pre-Hadrianic and three successive periods of building in stone.

A small section of the ramparts can be seen in the park to the east and a building (excavated in 1962) with a hypocaust, probably the home of the commandant, is also visible. It is on the premises of Mains Farm which lies opposite the church and permission to view can be obtained from the farmer. There is also a small museum on the site. The garrison of the fort is not known for certain but three different inscriptions suggest the 4th Cohort of Breuci or Brittones. One is shown below.

[MINER]- (?)
VÆ IVL. GER[MA]
NVS ACTAR[IVS] [2]
COH. IIII. BR[ITTONVM] (?)
ANTONINIA[NÆ]
V. S. LL. M.

To Miner-
va Julius Germa-
nus actarius of the
fourth cohort of Brittones
[styled] Antoniniana
. [dedicates this,] &c.

24

PLAN OF EBCHESTER,

Showing position of Roman Ramparts and Remains.

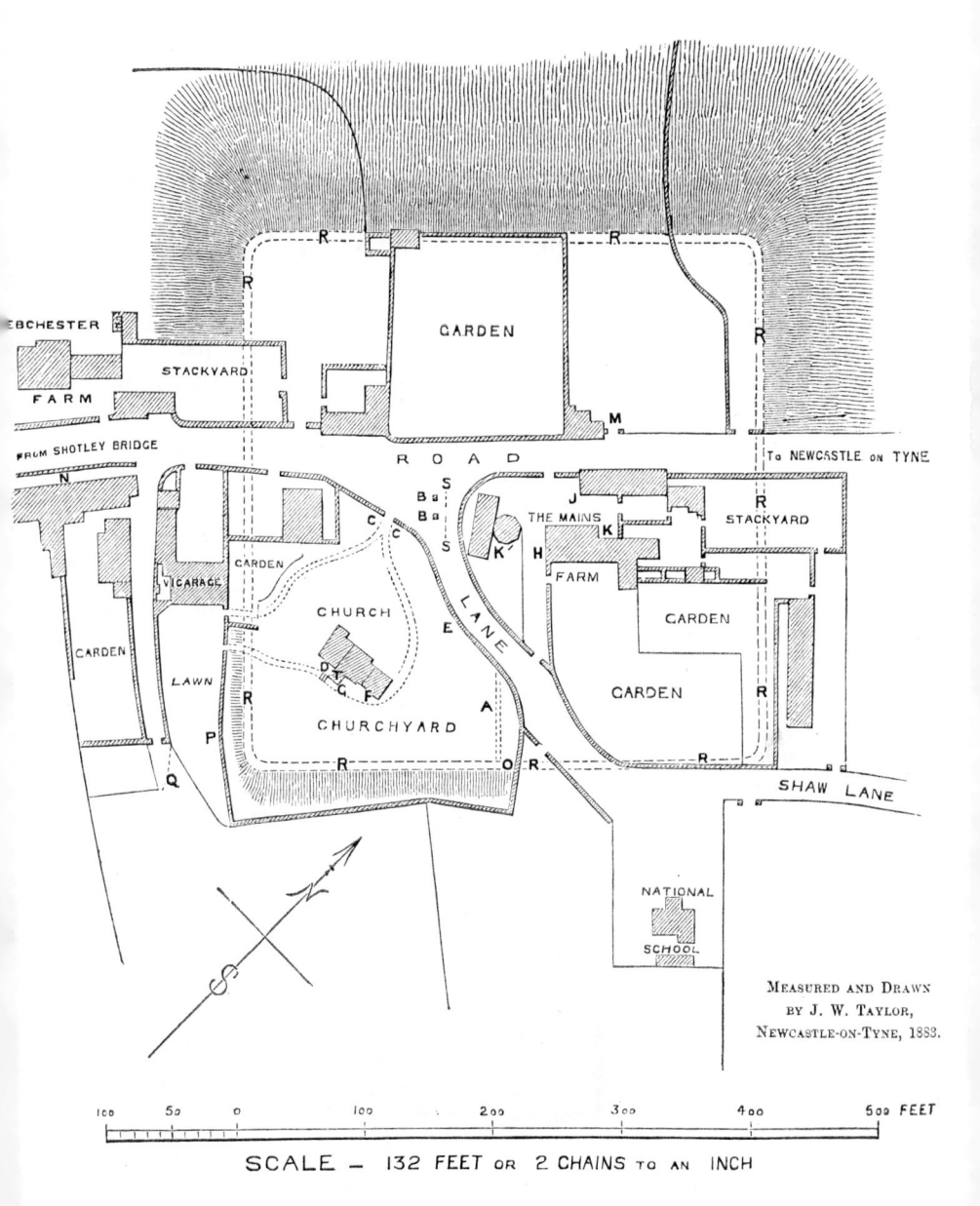

MEASURED AND DRAWN
BY J. W. TAYLOR,
NEWCASTLE-ON-TYNE, 1883.

SCALE — 132 FEET OR 2 CHAINS TO AN INCH

The following is an Explanation of the References on the Plan:—

    A. Line of Channeled stones taken up in 1876.
    B B. Bases of Doorjambs of Roman building found in 1876.
    C C. Present position of Bases.

D. Present position of Altar, found in foundations at west end of Church in 1876.
E. Present position of Sculptures built into Churchyard wall, found in 1876.
F. Altar forming jamb of window of Chancel.
G. Sculptured stones, built into retaining wall facing porch.

H J K K' M N. Sculptured stones, of various kinds, built into walls.
O. Probable position of Southern Gateway of Station.
P Q. Present positions of Channeled stones taken from A.
R R R R. Line of Ramparts of Station.
S S. Line of Draining Tiles taken up in 1876.
T. Porch of Church, containing many Sculptured stones, found in 1876 and previously, built into the inner walls.

Roger Gale in 1711 described Dere Street near Ebchester as it was in his day. "I looked", he wrote, "in a direct line along one of the most entire regular and large ways I ever saw and the ridge being for the most part two yards in height, full eight yards broad and all paved with stone that it is at present as even as new laid".

From Ebchester north, Dere Street follows the line of the modern road through Whittonstall to Castle Hill where a Roman fortlet guards the road. This Roman site is generally known as Apperley Dene. It was excavated in 1951. Horsley had been the first to notice the fortlet. "The Military Way", he wrote, "having crossed the Tyne proceeds towards Ebchester; about ½ mile north from Whittonstall is a remarkable turn in it, and at this turn an exploratory fort of about 30 yards square. The situation of it is high and the prospect large: and near it is a tumulus which I found to consist mainly of stones, covered with green turf".

Excavation showed the period of its occupation was brief and its use uncertain. It consisted of a square and possibly stone structure with an opening on to Dere Street surrounded by two ditches with a causeway in each.

During most of its route to Riding Mill, Dere Street follows the modern road or lies close to it. Sections can be seen near Broomley and in a wood at Riding Mill. It was also traced near the "Duke of Wellington". Through Farnley the two roads coincide, then Dere Street takes a more westerly line over Dilston Haughs with Corbridge Railway Station on the right, crossing the Tyne west of the present bridge.

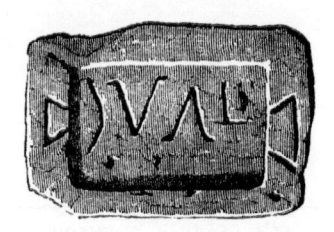

> VAL   Centuria Valerii.

Size, 1 ft. by 8 in.
A centurial stone from Ebchester.

FORT AT CHESTER-LE-STREET

The fort here is in a built-up area of the town and is mainly covered by the church and grammar school. At various times fragments of the fort have been discovered with coins, pottery and votive tablets. Scientific excavations of sections of the fort were conducted in 1869, 1963 and 1978. The conjectural plan of the fort here shown is based on the maps in Archaeologia Aeliana (1968) by G. P. Gillam and J. Tait and A.A. (1971) by J. S. Rainbird. It will save a complicated description of the parts already traced. Nothing of the fort can be seen today. On two sides it was defended by the Cong burn and the River Wear.

The name of the fort was *Concangium*. According to the Notitia Dignitatum it was garrisoned at some time by the *Numerus Vigilum Congangios*. The earliest pottery dates from the Antonine Period (138 to 161 A.D.) and the fort was probably built after the Antonine withdrawal from Scotland, when Hadrian's Wall was reoccupied. It covers an area of 6½ acres.

Concangium was on the road running from Brough (*Petuaria*) on the Humber to *Pons Aelius* (Newcastle) and as far as our knowledge goes was the only fort on this 100 mile road. It is probable there was a Roman bridge carrying this road north of the camp across the Cong burn because stones and Roman remains were found when the bank was being cemented in 1930. A branch left this road at Wrekenton for South Shields (*Arbeia*), and is known locally as the Wrekendyke. Binchester and Lanchester were also probably connected with Chester-le-Street by road.

DEO APOLLI-
NI LEG. II. A[VG.]

To the god Apollo
the second legion
[the august.

9 in. by 8 in.

DEAB[V]S
VET[ERI]BVS

To the
ancient
gods.

1 ft. 2 in. by 7 in.

10 in. by 6 in.

Three altars from Chester-le-Street. The first is to Apollo by an officer of the 2nd Legion whose name has been cut off. The second has some letters below which have been interpreted as **VEDRA**, the Roman name of the river Wear.

27

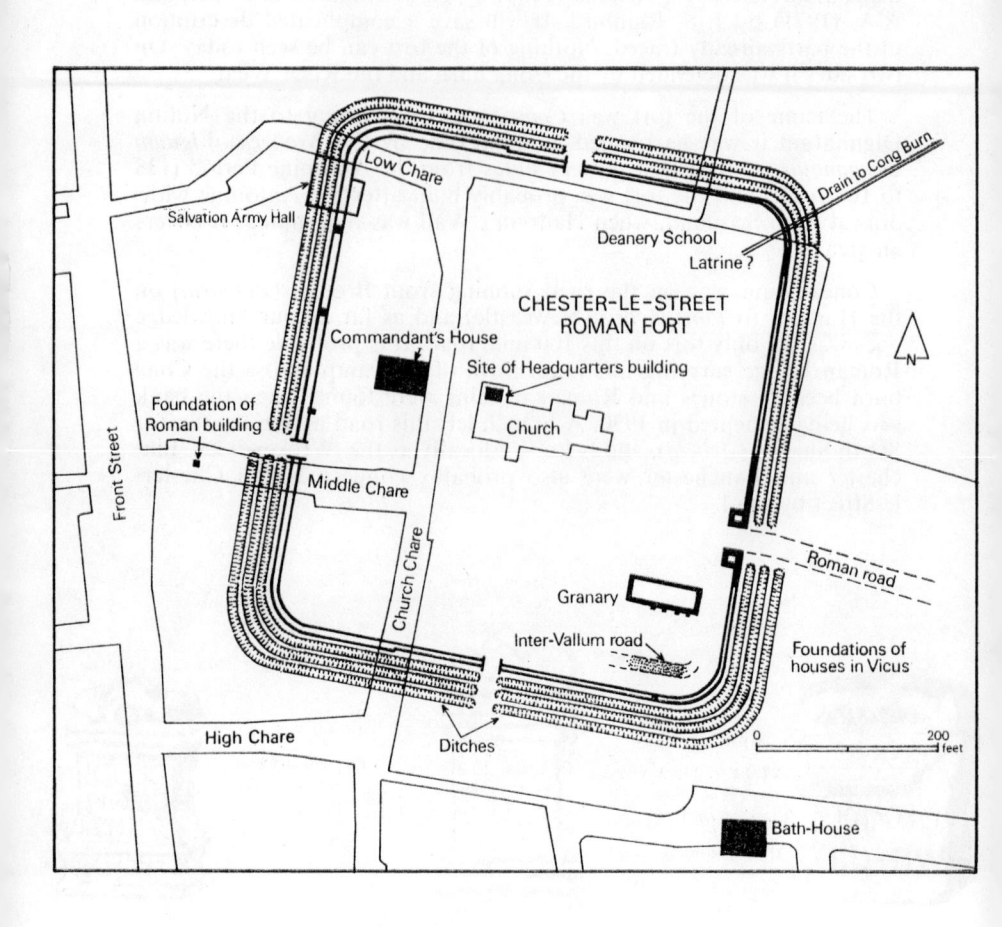

CHESTER-LE-STREET ROMAN FORT

Labels on map:
- Low Chare
- Salvation Army Hall
- Drain to Cong Burn
- Deanery School
- Latrine ?
- Commandant's House
- Site of Headquarters building
- Church
- Foundation of Roman building
- Front Street
- Middle Chare
- Church Chare
- Roman road
- Granary
- Inter-Vallum road
- Foundations of houses in Vicus
- High Chare
- Ditches
- Bath-House
- N
- 0   200 feet

SOUTH SHIELDS (Arbeia)

The early antiquarians provide us with little information about the fort here. Leland merely says: "Opposite to Tynemouth was a city ravaged by the Danes, *Urfa* by name where King Oswin was born." Camden does not mention it. At the end of the 17th century some Roman altars were found: a large and "elegantly carved" one is shown here.

Back of the Altar.   Size, 4 feet 2 inches by 2 feet 1 inch.

It is dedicated to Jupiter the Conservator on the occasion of the safe arrival of Caracalla and Geta at Rome. It can be dated to 211 or 212 A.D. The two emperors probably sailed from South Shields. Later the name Geta was erased. Horsley was really the first to realize there was a Roman site here. "The altars" he wrote, "that have been found here and the military way which has gone from it, are convincing proofs of this."

29

Roman ship passes Tynemouth on its way back to Rome.

R. S. Surtees in his *History of Durham* (Vol. 11 p.101) writes:—

There is no doubt that the Romans had some sort of establishment on the Luwe Hill, an eminence or rising ground immediately at the entrance into the Harbour . . . The Station seems to have included several acres and fragments of Roman bricks and pottery are turned up abundantly in a field adjoining the Lawe Hill when in tillage.

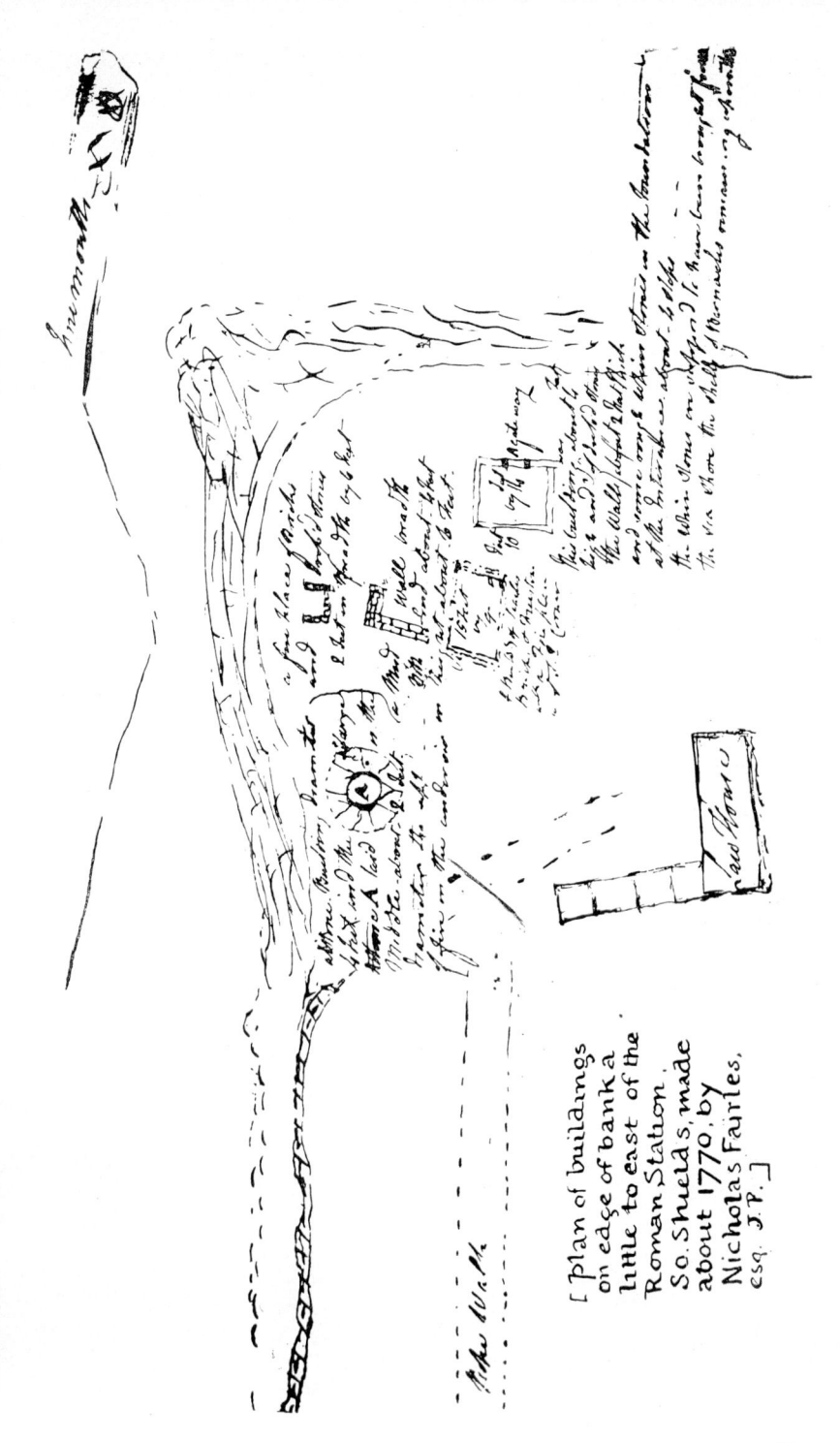

[Plan of buildings on edge of bank a little to east of the Roman Station, So. Shields, made about 1770, by Nicholas Fairles, esq. J.P.]

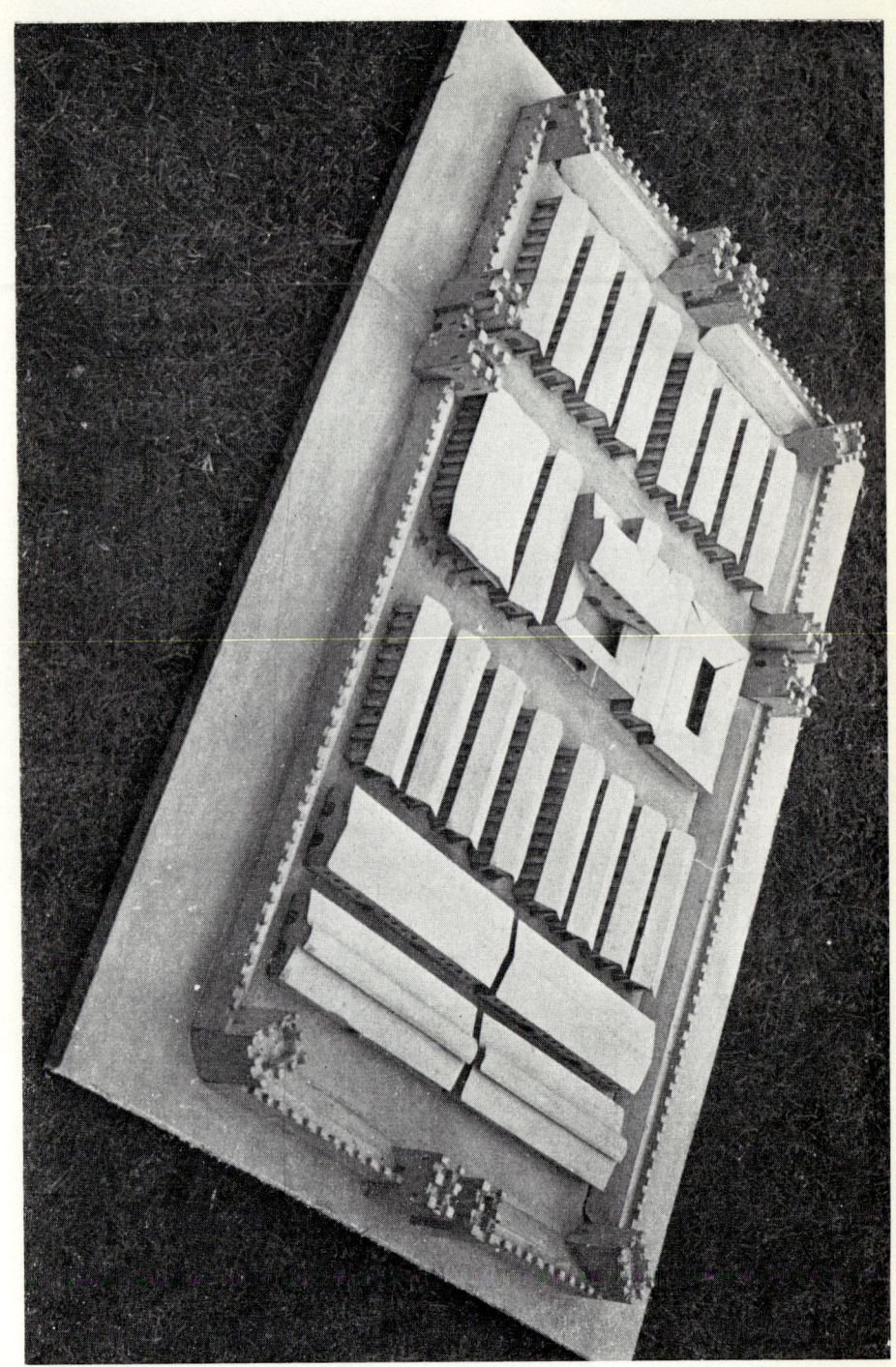

Arbeia — Reconstruction

As would be expected at a seaport there was a large and important civilian settlement here. Nicholas Fairless discovered a Roman hypocaust east of the fort "which consisted of brick and dressed freestone intermingled". His plan shows this bath-house with other buildings around.

Bruce had little to say about the fort at Shields but in the 2nd edition of his *Roman Wall* gives a good description of the site on the Lawe.

The ground on which it stands has the sea-cliff for its eastern boundary and the shore of the river for its northern. At some little distance inland, and at a lower level, it is protected by a stream called the Milldam which joins the Tyne, and was of more importance formerly than at present; the memory is still preserved of occasions, when the tide has risen so high as to insulate the promontory, and the distinction of the inhabitants into 'over-dammers' and 'under-dammers', as they lived on one side or other of the stream, is not entirely worn out . . . Few traces of Roman magnificence are now visible, but the bold south-west rampart of the station may easily be detected by proceeding up 'Fairless's old waggon-way', which cuts through it.

In 1874 a change took place. The land on which the fort stood was owned by the Ecclesiastical Commissioners who up till that time had only granted leases for 21 years which meant that the land remained under tillage. This policy was changed and the site was given over to housing. Before this happened however a substantial excavation was carried out and so important were the discoveries that a section of the site was preserved as *Roman Remains Park*. The houses built over a

The "Aqueduct Stone"

century ago have now been demolished and the site is now being excavated with modern techniques and eventually we should have here the only fort in Britain thoroughly excavated and preserved.

The fort was probably built about 128 A.D. in stone during the reign of Hadrian when the system of northern defences was being established as the Roman Wall. Pottery has suggested a Flavian origin but if so the fort must have been sited somewhere else on the hilltop. When Severus came north in 208 A.D. the fort was turned into a supply base with a very small garrison. Fourteen granaries have already been found. When the Scottish campaigns were over the fort returned to its former use and some of the granaries were changed into barracks. An inscription shown below records the building of a new aqueduct in 222 A.D. by the Fifth Cohort of Gauls.

The fort seems to have been abandoned late in the 3rd century and not used again until well into the 4th. The last coins found in the fort are two of the Emperor Arcadius who reigned from A.D. 395 to A.D. 408.

The original 2nd century garrison seems to have been a cavalry regiment the *ala Sabiniana*, 500 strong followed by the First Ala of Austurians (name mentioned on a tombstone). An inscription mentions the 5th Cohort of Gauls at the beginning of the 3rd century with, later in the 4th century, a Unit of Tigris Lightermen (numerous Barcariorum Tigrisensium) mentioned in the *Notitia* along with the name of the fort ARBEIA. They were probably only here for a short time since South Shields went out of use by *c.* 400 A.D.

The fort in its final form measures 620 by 360 feet covering an area of just over five acres. Its defences are a stone wall backed by a turf rampart with a gateway in each of its sides. In front are two ditches.

A very large collection of Roman material has come from the site. There are two magnificent funereal monuments. The one to Regina, with its inscription in two languages (unique in Britain), is shown here.

The first part of the inscription is in Latin and reads in translation—"To the divine shades. To Regina a freedwoman and (his) wife, Barates a Palmyrene (erected this monument. She was) by nation a Catuallaunian, (and lived) thirty years." It ends with a line in the Palmyrene language, translated—"Regina, freedwoman of Barates, alas!" Regina is shown with a distaff and spindle in one hand while the other raises a decorated chest supposed to hold her personal possessions. At the other side is a basket containing weaving materials. Barates was a merchant who supplied military standards and his own epitaph was found at Corbridge where he died aged 68 years.

It has been suggested by Dr. David Smith that this sculpture and the one following were the work of a Palmyrene living at South Shields.

The second funereal monument reads—"To the divine shades of Victor. He was by nation, a Moor, he lived twenty years, and was the freed man of Numerianus, a horseman of the first *ala* of the Astureans, who most affectionately followed (his former servant to the grave)."

ARBEIA

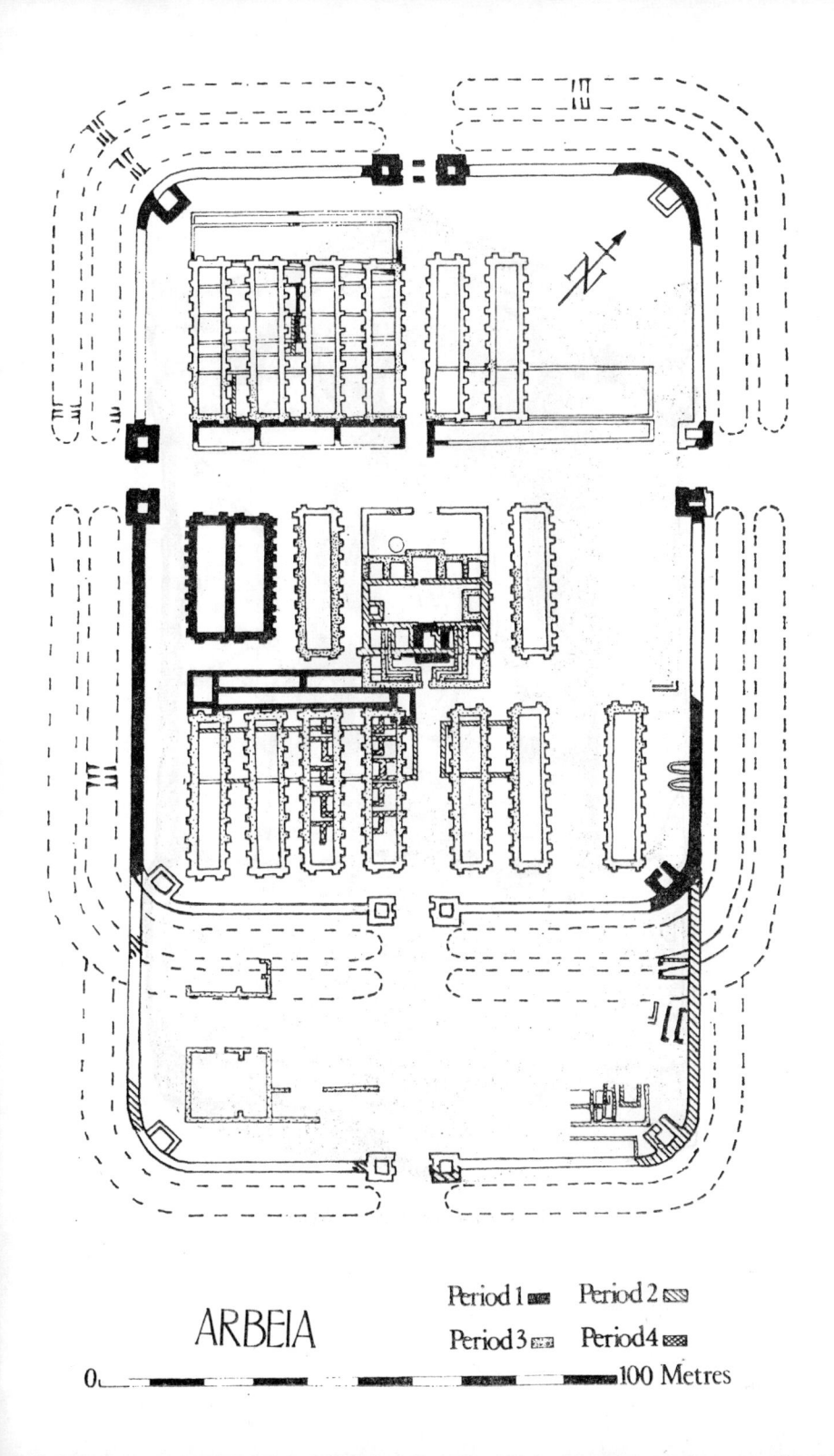

Period 1 Period 2
Period 3 Period 4

0   100 Metres

The funereal monument to Regine.

Monument to Victor the Moor.

South Shields has been the source of an amazing collection of stones and objects illustrating life on the Roman frontier. The important excavation now being carried out will undoubtedly reveal more treasures in the future. We here show some of the interesting finds.

37

Bronze checkpiece from helmet late 2nd century. The figure in the centre is one of the Dioscuri—Castor and Pallux (The companion checkpiece would have shown his brother). A dolphin is depicted below and there are leaf and floral motives.

Bone weaving frame. Perforated bone plate with silver mountings. Only $3\frac{1}{2}$ x $1\frac{1}{4}$ inches. It is a heddle-frame used for weaving narrow bands of material.

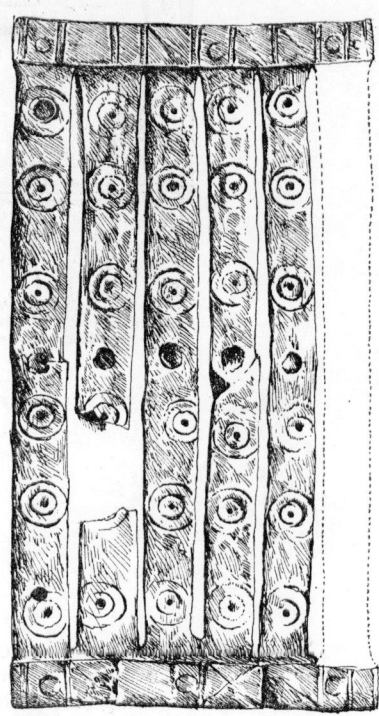

Altar to the goddess Brigantia by one Congennicus, discovered in 1959 on the parade ground which lay north-east of the fort

Roman skillet (*patera*) cast in bronze. Early 3rd century. Probably made in Gaul. Found in the wreck of a ship on the north sands at South Shields. *Paterae* were used for many purposes in Roman cookery, such as boiling stews and decocting wine, and sometimes had strainers. Each Roman soldier carried one.

THE ROMAN WALL

All these books are lavishly illustrated

HADRIAN'S WALL. Guide to the Central Sector by *Robin Birley*. Forty-eight pages. **60p**

THE ROMANS IN NORTH BRITAIN by *T. H. Rowland*. Sixty-four pages. **80p**

THE ARMY OF HADRIAN'S WALL by *Brian Dobson* and *David Breeze*. Forty-eight pages. **60p**

BUILDING THE ROMAN WALL by *Brian Dobson* and *David Breeze*. Revised and with new illustrations. **60p**

CIVILIANS ON THE ROMAN WALL by *Robin Birley*. Sixty-four pages. Illustrated. **£1**

SHORT GUIDE TO THE ROMAN WALL. Fifty-six pages. A detailed and up to date guide with numerous maps. Remarkable value. By *T. H. Rowland*. Illustrated in colour. **60p**

HOUSESTEADS ROMAN FORT by *R. Birley*. Four pages in colour. **35p**

CHARTS OF ROMAN WALL. A series of magnificent coloured reconstructions of the Roman Wall. Size seventeen inches by twenty-five inches. Price **70p** each.

1. **South Gate, Housesteads.**
2. **Mansio or Inn at Vindolanda.**
3. **Latrines at Housesteads.**

VINDOLANDA IN COLOUR. A magnificent souvenir of the Roman fort and settlement which has attracted so much attention recently. **80p**

THE ROMAN WALL RECONSTRUCTED. Twelve magnificent paintings in full colour showing the Roman Wall as it was when built. Paintings by *R. Embleton*. Text by *C. M. Daniels*. **80p**

DERE STREET. Roman Road North by *T. H. Rowland*. From York to Scotland. **70p**

HOUSESTEADS IN THE DAYS OF THE ROMANS by *R. Embleton*. Colour. **60p**

WHAT THE SOLDIERS WORE ON HADRIAN'S WALL by *H. Russell Robinson*. Colour. **£1**

BIRDOSWALD FORT by *Peter Howard*. **60p**

VINDOLANDA JEWELLERY by *Martin Henig*. **60p**

VINDOLANDA WRITING TABLETS by *A. Bowman* and *J. Thomas*. **60p**